T0125866

THE NIGHT
IN GETHSEMANE

Massimo Recalcati

THE NIGHT
IN GETHSEMANE

*Translated from the Italian
by Ann Goldstein*

Europa
editions

Europa Editions
214 West 29th Street
New York, N.Y. 10001
www.europaeditions.com
info@europaeditions.com

Copyright © 2019 by Giulio Einaudi editore s.p.a. Torino
First publication 2020 by Europa Editions

Translation by Ann Goldstein
Original title: *La notte del Getsemani*
Translation copyright 2020 by Europa Editions

All rights reserved, including the right of reproduction
in whole or in part in any form.

Library of Congress Cataloging in Publication Data is available
ISBN 978-1-60945-622-1

Recalcati, Massimo
The Night in Gethsemane

Book design by Emanuele Ragnisco
www.mekkanografici.com

Cover image: *The Kiss of Judas* by Giotto di Bondone c. 1305 Fresco,
Scrovegni Chapel, Padua. Photo: Alamy Stock Photo

Prepress by Grafica Punto Print – Rome

Printed in the USA

CONTENTS

THE NIGHT
IN GETHSEMANE

INTRODUCTION

Then all the disciples deserted him and fled.
—MATTHEW 26:56

During the night in Gethsemane Jesus is at his most deeply human. This night speaks to us more about the vulnerability of Christ's life, its finiteness, than it does about crucifixion; it's about us, about our human condition.

The spotlight is not on the symbol of the cross and the unprecedented violence of torment, torture, and death. During the night in Gethsemane the tragic finale does not yet afflict Christ's body but, rather, pierces his soul. There are no nails or scourges, no crown of thorns or blows; there is only the weight of a night that will never end, the helpless, bewildered solitude of the life that experiences betrayal and abandonment. This is the night of man, not the night of God. In the course of this night the true passion of Christ is played out: God withdraws into the deep silence of Heaven, refusing to spare his only beloved son the traumatic experience of a fall, of absolute abandonment. The disciples alone remain with him, but, rather than share his anguish, they fall asleep or, like Peter, the most faithful among them, testify falsely on his name, denying him. Jesus is left alone with the soldiers and the temple priests, who want him captured and dead.

The glory of the Messiah, hailed as he joyously enters

Jerusalem, is transformed abruptly into an experience of intense solitude. Jesus is accused of a theological outrage: dragging God toward man, confusing what is lacking in man with what is lacking in God; exposing man to a world without God, to the absolute freedom of the creature pushed to the limits of his irreducible distance from God.

During the night in Gethsemane, Jesus doesn't appear to be the son of God; he's a delinquent, a common criminal, a blasphemer. No miracle can save him; his life is revealed in a tragic edict of extreme helplessness. What's important is not the experience of God's speech—the word of the Father who comes to the aid of his son—but God's deathless silence, his infinite distance from the son who has been handed over to the wounds of betrayal, political intrigue, the fall, the irreversible, harrowing approach of death.

This book is an attempt to illuminate the scene of Gethsemane in all its details. But why return to the night in Gethsemane? And why, in particular, should a psychoanalyst do so? For me—or rather *in myself*—the answer is clear: because in this scene the biblical text speaks radically about man, touches the essence of his condition, the condition of man "without God," his frailty, his lack, his torments. Aren't the wounds of abandonment and betrayal and the wound of the inevitability of death perhaps the deepest wounds that man has to endure? Isn't it here that the most radical dimension of a "negative" that no dialectic can redeem is manifested? And doesn't psychoanalysis constantly confront in its practice and theory this tragic and "negative" dimension of life?

Regardless, in the dark hours of this night we encounter not only our suffering as human beings but also a decisive sign that we must try to deal in an affirmative way with the unavoidable weight of the "negative." This is what I call the "second prayer" of Jesus. The night in Gethsemane is not, in fact, solely a night of utter abandonment and betrayal, of submissiveness to God's silence and to the violence of arrest; it is also a night of prayer. But Jesus doesn't have just one way of praying. During that night he encounters the deepest roots of prayer. And only through this experience of prayer is he able to find an opening that allows him to endure this terrible night: prayer that is not so much an appeal addressed to the Other—a request for help and consolation, an entreaty—but prayer that is the handing over of himself to his own destiny, to the singular Law of his own desire. Isn't this perhaps the ultimate, most profound, and unexpected meaning of Gethsemane? And isn't this what's at stake on every human pathway in life?

It's the crucial point where, in my view, the lesson of Gethsemane meets the lesson of psychoanalysis: we coincide with our own destiny, decide to give ourselves to our own story, since only in that giving can we uniquely rewrite it, and welcome the otherness of the Law that inhabits us, taking on our condition of lack not as an affliction but as an encounter with what we most intensely are.

Valchiusella, January 2019

This book has its origin in a talk I gave at the Bose Monastic Community on February 25, 2017, under the title *The Lesson of Gethsemane*.

To my sisters and brothers
in the Bose Monastic Community

THE FAULT OF THE PRIESTS

I n the story told by the Gospels, the experience of the night in Gethsemane opens the cycle of the Passion of Christ. Behind him is the joyous entry into Jerusalem, the light of the city that jubilantly welcomes its Messiah. Unarmed, sitting on a donkey and a colt, "the foal of a donkey," as Matthew recounts (Matthew 21:5), Jesus of Nazareth enters through the gates of the city. The people, the same who will later, at the time of the Passion, stridently call for his death with hatred-charged violence, welcome him joyously, exalting his glory:

> Most of the crowd spread their garments on the road, and others cut branches from the trees and spread them on the road. And the crowds that went before him and that followed him shouted, "Hosanna to the Son of David! Blessed is he who comes in the name of the Lord! Hosanna in the highest!" (Matthew 21:8–9)

During the period between the enthusiastic Hosanna and the dark anguish of Gethsemane, Jesus' preaching becomes harsher and more radical. Christian subversiveness collides with the codified religion of the priests and their more traditional symbols, including the Temple of Jerusalem. Here we touch on a key point in Jesus' experience:

the power of speech animated by faith tends to clash with its institutionalization. It's a theme that has been taken up forcefully in psychoanalysis by Wilfred Bion and Elvio Fachinelli: the *mystical* always comes into conflict with the *religious*. The thrust of desire and the passion for truth inevitably clash with the institution, which stubbornly defends and preserves its own identity so as to avoid any form of contamination. At the same time, when the free force of speech is institutionalized—is rigidly regimented into an established code—it risks losing its generative power. The history of religions and of every type of School testifies to this: when a doctrine is institutionalized it tends to lose the authentic thrust of desire and the capacity for opening up. Institutionalization coincides with a movement of closure in contrast with the movement of the words, which aspire instead to open up and expand. "Organizing," as Pasolini would say, prevails in the end over the propulsive thrust of "transhumanizing."[1] That's why the chief priests of the temple, the scribes and teachers of the Law, become the preferred targets of Jesus' anger. Entering the Temple, which has become a place of commerce and degradation, he, as Matthew tells us, "drove out all who sold and bought in the temple, and he overturned the tables of the money-changers and the seats of those who sold pigeons" (Matthew 21:12).

Jesus empties the Temple of the objects and idols that fill it, he cleanses it, reopens its "central place" so that it can continue to be a house of prayer. Prayer exists only if

---

[1] Pier Paolo Pasolini, *Trasumanar e organizzar* [Transhumanize and Organize] (Milan: Garzanti, 1971).

there is a "central place," an experience of emptiness, if the fetishistic presence of the object is eliminated.[2] For this reason the institutionalization of faith always carries the risk that it will be assimilated into a formal code of behavior, as the Gospels vividly describe through the image of the sterile fig tree incapable of producing fruit (Matthew 21:18–22). Not surprisingly, Lacan likens Jesus to Socrates, starting precisely from the subversive power of their speech, which can open a breach in the life of the city.[3]

The fault of the temple priests is that they represent a faith that has forgotten itself, that has lost contact with the potency of desire, that has grown sterile in the exercise of power; they haven't properly interpreted the stakes of inheritance. Who is a just heir? What does it mean to inherit? What does inheritance of the Law mean? Here is the priests' greatest fault: they have interpreted inheritance solely as continuity, as formal replication, as ritual repetition of the Same, crushing it through pure conservation of the past. They are, in Jesus' famous words, "whitewashed tombs, which outwardly appear beautiful, but within they are full of dead men's bones and all uncleanness" (Matthew 23:27).

Authentic inheritance of the Law—the inheritance of Abraham, Isaac, and Jacob—doesn't consist of repeating it, cloning it, preserving and thus killing it. Rather,

[2] Jacques Lacan, *The Seminar. Book VII. The Ethics of Psychoanalysis* (New York: Norton, 1997).
[3] Ibid. *The Seminar. Book VIII. Transference* (Cambridge: Polity, 2015).

inheritance implies a forward movement that aims at fulfilling the Law without reducing it to a dead body. In a harsh parable that Jesus recounts right inside the city walls, the temple priests are likened to the tenant farmers who don't recognize that the vineyard where they work belongs to their landlord. These tenants don't respect the rental contract that they have drawn up with the legitimate owner of the vineyard, and they kill and mistreat the servants who are sent during harvest time to collect the share due to the owner (Matthew 21:33–36).

Inheritance implies a discontinuity within the continuity, whereas the murderous tenants claim an obscure property right, ignoring every form of symbolic debt. They forget the origin of the land they work, they forget the symbolic agreement that binds them to the owner of the vineyard. Thus they are bad heirs: they want to possess their inheritance rather than recognize that inheritance is above all a relationship with our origins, and implies a responsibility to cultivate what we have received from the Other but without ignoring the debt.

Faced with the violence of the tenants who have killed his servants, the owner decides to send his only son to collect the share of the fruits of the farm that is due him, and in the conviction that against his son—the legitimate heir—they wouldn't dare perpetrate the same violence. But the tenants take this opportunity to seize the inheritance definitively by ruthlessly killing the owner's son (Matthew 21:37–39). The theological-political metaphor is very clear: the temple priests are like the murderous tenants who brutally eviscerate the complex process of inheritance and usurp the highest meaning of the Law, pursuing their own interests *against* the Law's. For this reason the parable concludes with a warning: "When therefore the owner of the vineyard comes, what will he do to those tenants?" (Matthew 21:40).

What is the more properly ethical meaning of this parable? To be just heirs we have to recognize the symbolic debt that binds us to our origin. The just heir works the land he has received with the freedom to produce new fruits. But if the debt is ignored, if inheritance becomes appropriation or usurpation, if the debt is "betrayed," nothing is produced; there is only death, and the transmission becomes the transmission of violence alone.

It's no coincidence that Jesus tells this parable shortly before the night in Gethsemane. In the tenants' brutal killing of the just heir he demonstrates the inevitability of his fate. The Pharisees and the scribes reject Jesus' speech; they experience it as a threat. They don't answer the call, they don't welcome the arrival of the just heir among them. They hold tight to their properties without acknowledging the symbolic debt that binds them to the father. They kill the just heir in order not to lose their power; they harden the defense of their identity rather than welcome he who comes to bring a new image of the Law. Their orthodoxy is nothing but a sterile fig tree, a dead field, the absence of desire as the leaven that alone can restore life to the Law, and without which the Law is nothing but a "heavy burden" laid "on men's shoulders" (Matthew 23:4), a weight that, requiring sacrifice, oppresses life.

In reality only the call of desire—incarnated by Jesus—can promise to free life from the sacrificial weight of the Law: "Come unto me, all who labor and are heavy laden, and I will give you rest" (Matthew 11:28).

A WATERSHED

The glory of the Hosanna that welcomed Jesus upon his entrance into Jerusalem fades rapidly during the dark night of Gethsemane, which marks the start of the Passion. According to the Scriptures, at the origin of this dramatic event is Jesus' betrayal by Judas. Between that betrayal and when we find Jesus in the garden of Gethsemane comes the heartbreaking rite of the Last Supper; here the act that Judas is about to carry out is revealed, and it will end finally in the garden of Gethsemane, with the recognition and arrest of Jesus.

The night in Gethsemane is a watershed in Jesus' life story. Never before had he been so unequivocally confronted with his own vulnerability; never before had he come up against the finite character of his human existence. The unique and subversive power of his speech seems to die, the phenomenal determination that has driven him to perform every sort of miracle seems to be exhausted, the beauty of the life he has tasted in all its forms seems to have come to an end.

The hour of Gethsemane is the hour of the fall of God, or, rather, it's the hour in which the Christian God is revealed to be "only a man," radically damaged by the negative. The hour of Gethsemane is not the hour of God but the hour of man. It's the hour in which God appears stripped naked: the hour of the fall of his glory. The events that follow Gethsemane seem to have been already written: the capture, the encounter with the priests of the Sanhedrin, the trial with Pilate, Calvary, crucifixion, and death. The palms that accompany the triumphal entry into Jerusalem are transformed into the weapons—swords and clubs—of the soldiers who in the darkness of Gethsemane arrest Jesus as if he were an ordinary criminal.

To begin to read the night in Gethsemane we have to contrast the scene of Jesus' entrance into Jerusalem, where he is welcomed by a jubilant populace, with Gethsemane, when, Luke writes, "his sweat became like great drops of blood falling down upon the ground" (Luke 22:44). We must insist on the dramaturgical opposition between the scene of Jesus' entrance into Jerusalem, where, his face illuminated by the sun, he is surrounded by people rejoicing, and the sweat that becomes blood, the face crushed to the ground in prayer, in despair, during the night in Gethsemane. We must hold fast to this unmediated opposition, which creates a discontinuity between the daylight of the Hosanna and the darkness of that night. No synthesis, no continuity, no progression is possible: rather, a tear, a laceration, a division. As night falls on the light of day, so silence and anguish seem to replace celebration of the Messiah.

It is no longer time for the speech that provokes outrage by preaching the disturbing truth of God who comes into the world to defend the least among us and the humble, of a Law that requires not revenge or punishment but freedom from sacrifice and the fear of death. In order to be believable, the preaching must now find its truth by means of testimony. From Jesus' perspective, there is, in effect, no possible truth without its testimony. That means that the truth of the Word consists in its incarnation alone. It's the radical ethical hermeneutics of Christianity: the letter without testimony is a dead letter; without heart—without desire—the meaning of the Law can't be understood.

The night in Gethsemane confines the fire of Jesus' speech in a corner. Is it really possible to overcome anguish, to escape its weight, to internalize the Law of one's own desire while rejecting the Law's oppressive demand for sacrifice? Is it possible to testify to the power of the Word in the face of death?

The truth of speech is not a theoretical, general abstract universal truth. During the night in Gethsemane Jesus puts *his own* speech to the test: puts it to the extreme test of anguish. Not surprisingly, for Lacan anguish always implies the subject's confrontation with his own desire; it's the subject's most radical translation of desire.[4]

Not until the solitary journey through this interminable night does Jesus' speech find its highest expression. If, in his last parables and preachings in Jerusalem, the fire of his speech blazed fiercely in the invectives against the so-called teachers of the Law and in the evocation of another possible form of the Law—freed from the inhuman weight of the Law—now, during the night in Gethsemane, there is only silence. Parable and preaching yield to prayer.

Jesus is called to bear witness to the truth of his own speech. If he hadn't been through the night in Gethsemane,

---

[4] Ibid. *The Seminar. Book X. Anxiety* (Cambridge: Polity, 2014).

the fall, and abandonment by God, by his friends, and by his disciples, if he hadn't, Lacan would say, experienced the nonexistence of the Other of the Other, would the truth of his speech have had the same force?

Isn't it starting precisely from this night—from the night in Gethsemane—that the testimony of the truth acquires all its value? Isn't it precisely this night that illuminates the power of Jesus' speech? Didn't he come to show men—to show all sinners—that it's possible to live without being crushed by fear of the Law or by fear of death? Isn't death the most pitiless face of the Law? Isn't the passage through this phantom of sacrifice what is most at stake in Gethsemane? Is it possible to have a Law that is not weight, oppression, death? Is it possible that the Law might be allied with the life of desire and not hostile to it? Is it possible to free the Law from its purely dutiful face?[5]

---

[5] All these questions are central in my *Contro il sacrificio. Al di là del fantasma sacrificale* [Against Sacrifice. Beyond the Phantom of Sacrifice] (Milan: Raffaello Cortina, 2017).

THE FALL

The night in Gethsemane opens with Jesus announcing to his disciples that his Passion and death are at hand, and that all of them will betray him, including, in particular, his most faithful disciple, Peter, to whom Jesus has entrusted the legacy of his teaching. As the night goes on, Jesus sinks into his time of anguish, intense solitude, and prayer. The night ends, finally, with the kiss of Judas and the arrest of Jesus.

In this sequence we can grasp the progressive metamorphosis that we have already noted: the glory of the Messiah hailed as he enters Jerusalem gives way to the brutality of arrest, as if Jesus had become a public menace, a criminal, a man who attacks the Law. No one seems to remember anything of what he said and did before. The fall of his glory into dust seems to erase every memory. We've had this experience in our own lives: the moment of success and acclaim is quickly forgotten; the glory of the Messiah is depleted by the inexorable violence of his fall.

Nonetheless, the power of the Christian lesson consists in thinking that only those who know the fall can know the glory. This means that the fullness of life can't be separated from the fatal encounter with the "negative" whose ultimate expression is death. This is the narrow gate through which Jesus himself—who, not surprisingly, says that he is "a gate"[6]—has to pass. But here it's not just a matter of leading one's sheep through the gate of the sheepfold, as the good shepherd does. In Gethsemane being a gate imposes the experience of testifying. It's no longer only a statement, a story, a narrative. Jesus is called on to become the gate by his own desire; Gethsemane is a necessary step where the power of speech meets its ultimate trial. It is where "speaking" remains joined through testimony to "doing," contrary to what happens to the teachers of the Law, because, contradicting the logic of testimony, "they preach but do not practice" (Matthew 23:1–12). Separating the truth of the speech from its necessary incarnation, the priests represent the insubstantial truth of a doctrine that is trapped in erudition, sterile, concerned with worship, with form. The experience of the night in Gethsemane shows in a different way that Jesus' speech maintains a special relationship with the truth. It says what it does; it doesn't separate saying from doing.

Only the testimony of singular "doing" can demonstrate the close relationship—internal and not external—between "saying" and truth. In Gethsemane Jesus experiences the Word that has to become flesh, that has to give testimony of its truth. Jesus is aiming at this testimony, not certainly at masochistic obedience to a Law that would require solely the sacrifice of his life.

But how important is it to maintain the tension between our "saying" and our "doing"? Isn't that a Christian definition of an ethical life? Striving to make "saying" coincide

---

[6] "I am the gate; whoever enters through me will be saved. They will come in and go out, and find pasture" (John 10:9).

with "doing," to think of truth as a singular act of testimony. Values do not exist on a disembodied, transcendental plane: they are not abstract generalities. Their only form of existence is to be incarnated in the acts of an "irreplaceable singularity." Only, in fact, starting from this "irreplaceability," as Derrida correctly states, "can one speak of the responsible subject."[7]

The idea here is that passing through a narrow gate allows us to realize a life that is richer, more productive, more vibrant, a life characterized by great "abundance" (John 10:1–21). Responsibility doesn't mean life crushed under the weight of the Law of duty; it is the appropriation of one's own desire, of the Law of one's own desire. A gate allows us to pass through to a new life, freed from the curse of the Law. For this reason Jesus says of himself that he is a gate, he identifies with that position, with the act of "becoming a gate." But not on a purely theoretical, speculative level. His life bears witness to what it means to become a gate, or, rather, what it means to pass through the gate that each person is for him- or herself: Jesus offers us the possibility of converting our life into a life that is more vibrant, richer, more productive.

In the Passion there is no trace of sacrifice, no genuflection before the Law, because, as we'll see later, it's in the name of the Law—the Law of his own desire—that Jesus passes through the gate that leads beyond the phantom of sacrifice and the fear of death. Thus he carries life beyond death, beyond anguish in the face of the Law and death.

---

[7] Jacques Derrida, *The Gift of Death* (Chicago: University of Chicago Press, 1995).

The old Law is in fact an image of degradation: it is itself death. The new life whose existence Jesus has preached is a life dominated neither by fear of the Law nor by fear of death. Jesus, in Gethsemane, becomes the very event of the *gate* that allows life to pass beyond the anguish of death and the Law such that death itself—beyond the phantom that makes us tremble before it—can become the occasion for an affirmative transformation of life: "Unless a grain of wheat falls into the earth and dies, it remains alone; but if it dies, it bears much fruit" (John 12:24). In this way Jesus can offer his life as if it were truly a gate, he can be the first to pass through fear of death and of the Law. In that sense the terrible cycle of his Passion is governed not by the economy of sacrifice but, rather, by the boundless gift of himself.

If the economy of sacrifice is in effect a shrewd economy of redemption and unlimited reparation, the gate of Jesus introduces us to a different economy, an economy of abundance and desire. The decision Jesus makes in Gethsemane is not to sacrifice his life on the grim altar of the Law but to offer, to give his life, to remain faithful to his own desire.[8] It's a gesture of absolute freedom whose foundation is in itself alone. Every act of love, if it is truly such, is absolute because it finds its satisfaction only in the fulfillment of itself and not in a personal advantage that might be gained at a later time. In Jesus' decision to go to the end, to fulfill his own destiny, we should perceive not

---

[8] For a closer examination of all these subjects, I refer the reader again to Recalcati, *Contro il sacrificio*, op. cit.

a sacrifice and renunciation of himself but, rather, the complete fulfillment of himself, because, as he says, "No one takes it [life] from me, but I lay it down of my own accord" (John 10:18).

THE TRAUMA OF BETRAYAL

D uring the night in Gethsemane Jesus confronts three radical experiences: betrayal, anguish in the face of his own death, and, finally, solitude and prayer.

The night in Gethsemane is the night of betrayal. The figures who embody it are notoriously two, apparently distant from and antithetical to one another. These are Judas and Peter. They are united above all by the fact that both are included among the twelve disciples, among the chosen. They're two of Jesus' most cherished students, his apostles, his traveling companions, Judas Iscariot no less than Peter. They're among those who are closest to Jesus. The figure of the friend, the brother, the disciple. This means that the most profound experience of betrayal comes not from a stranger but from someone who is close to us, the closest—someone in whom we place our full trust.

A stranger's "betrayal" has the nature of a mere deception. Deception doesn't imply any love, any intimacy, any closeness. It's a purely cynical stratagem. Someone who plots a deception has no affective bond with the person he deceives. His act responds only and exclusively to personal gain. No symbolic pact has to be broken, no love damaged. The author of the deception works lucidly, without passion, without any emotional obstacle, because in his eyes the deceived person has no value.

We can truly betray only those who are closest to us—the friend, the brother, the beloved, the teacher—those to whom we are bound by an agreement based on speech: "You are my woman," "You are my teacher," "You are my friend." True betrayal, unlike deception, shatters a symbolic pact based on the law of speech. Thus betrayal always has the nature of a trauma. It's not the stranger who betrays, because the betrayer has to have a particular intimacy with the betrayed; the betrayer is not the outsider but, as Jesus teaches, the one who puts his hand in the plate we're eating from. The only true betrayal is betrayal of our nearest: the student betrays his teacher or the teacher his student, the beloved man betrays the beloved woman, the beloved woman the beloved man. We can, in short, betray only those who have recognized us as essential for their life: our own teacher, our own friend, our own beloved.

It's one of the twelve, Jesus says: "one of you will betray me" (John 13:21). It's not the temple priests who betray him; it's his friends, his traveling companions, his most cherished, most intimate students. Jesus has the experience that a teacher often has: those who have loved him turn their backs, abandon him precisely in the hour of his need, the hour when his glory is tarnished, when his name—the name of the teacher—has become an "outrage."

The Betrayal of Judas

The biblical text situates betrayal in a primal scene: the first betrayal is Adam and Eve's betrayal of God. The serpent intimates that the limit God has imposed on humans—that they are not to approach the tree of knowledge—serves in reality to safeguard God's own privileges and his egotistical pleasure. Every symbolic debt toward the Creator is cancelled out in the name of the right to the freedom to enjoy that Adam and Eve—driven by the serpent's malice—claim. God is not the one to whom they owe their life but an impediment to their life.[9]

The "betrayer" refuses to acknowledge the symbolic debt that binds him to the "betrayed"; as the primal scene of Adam and Eve clearly demonstrates, the betrayed has become for the betrayer an obstacle to the affirmation of his own life, a burdensome weight to be dropped, to get free of as quickly as possible.

During the night in Gethsemane, however, the scene of betrayal is repeated in a form that is much richer in nuance than the original scene of Adam and Eve's betrayal. The betrayers, Judas and Peter, are not similar figures, like

---

[9] Genesis 3:1–13. The commentary of Pierangelo Sequeri was crucial for these verses. See his *Il timore di Dio* [The Fear of God] (Milan: Vita e Pensiero, 1993).

Adam and Eve, and, not surprisingly, their betrayals will have profoundly different results. During the Last Supper, as the moment of betrayal approaches, Jesus states that the betrayer is not outside of us but within us, *among us, one of us, near us.* He has eaten with us, has shared the table with us: "The hand of him who betrays me," says Jesus, "is with me on the table" (Luke 22:21).

What is more intimate than eating together, sharing the same table, eating from the same plate? The betrayer doesn't come from another house; he lives in our house. The Last Supper is the last because someone has betrayed, has broken the symbolic pact that bound the twelve, has dissolved the symbolic companionship of being at the table together. The life of the community of disciples and their Teacher is no longer possible, since the pact based on speech has been shattered. This is how Jesus evokes the figure of Judas. He's one of you, he's one of us, he's close to us, he's not an enemy but a friend, a brother, a disciple. The anguish then spreads like a specter among the disciples: looking at one another in bewilderment, they wonder, who is the traitor? The Passover celebration is transformed into a nightmare: *who among us has betrayed the Teacher?*

I must insist on the scene of this betrayal, which takes place during the dinner that celebrates Passover. It's an intimate dinner, at which the Teacher shares the table with his disciples. This fact is not insignificant: the betrayal occurs while bread is shared, while Jesus and the disciples are eating together, during the intimacy of the meal. Indeed, John reports that Jesus recognizes Judas as the betrayer while he invites him to eat a mouthful of bread dipped in his own plate (John 13:18–30). Mark repeats it: the traitor is "one of the twelve, one who is dipping bread into the dish with me" (Mark 14:20). The traitor eats from the same plate as the teacher; he is nourished on his speech, has benefitted from his teaching, has shared the same table. And now he wants to destroy his teacher, he spits on the speech that has shaped him, shows no gratitude for what he has received, recognizes no form of debt.

Thus Judas is a figure very different from the accusers of Socrates as they are described by Plato in the *Apologia of Socrates*. There, too, a teacher faced with the possibility of dying in the name of truth decides not to retreat. Socrates in fact offers his life to demonstrate that the search for truth cannot be abandoned. Not even the fear of death can damage the teacher's consistency. What's most important is not living but responding to our own desire. What's most important is not "weighing up the prospects of life and death" but whether we are acting "justly or unjustly," whether care for our souls counts more than care for our bodies or possessions.[10]

Socrates shares nothing with his implacable accusers. No dinner, no breaking of the pact, no betrayal. Socrates is deviously accused of corrupting the youth of Athens by men who fear—as the priests fear Jesus—the excessive influence of the teacher's subversive speech in the life of the city. Certainly the slander against him recalls what Jesus, too, had to suffer. Socrates, rather than renounce the truth of his speech, chooses to renounce his life.

[10] Plato, *Apologia of Socrates*, in *The Last Days of Socrates* (London: Penguin Books, 2003), p. 54.

Nonetheless, his ethical choice does not involve the trauma of betrayal the way Jesus experienced it.

For Jesus what is central during the night in Gethsemane is the very human experience of betrayal, not, as for Socrates, the ethical opposition between the Law of speech and the Law of the city. While the story of Socrates concludes with the epic act of the teacher who drinks the cup of hemlock to testify, up to his last breath, to the irreducible value of his own speech, which is devoted to the search for truth, Jesus' last supper ends with Judas going off into the night after having intimately betrayed his teacher. The passion of Jesus doesn't end with Judas' act but begins there. While Socrates' final act raises the figure of the teacher to the glorious dignity of an icon in a gesture that will honor the divine dimension of the truth, Judas, selling the life of his teacher for a mere thirty pieces of silver—the sum needed at the time to buy a slave—degrades Jesus to a common criminal. In the first case we have an elevation of the Teacher, in the second his humiliation.

But what determined Judas' betrayal? Like all the other disciples, he was profoundly in love with Jesus. The life of his teacher was for him, as for all his brothers, a magnet that polarized his own life. Jesus' speech had the force of an irresistible call. Jesus is a teacher who knows how to inspire great passions. He inspires love and desire in those who listen to his speech. And desire, as Lacan notes, is an eccentric and subversive force that provokes "a permanent disorder in a body subjected to the statutes of adaptation."[11] In psychoanalysis we speak of the capacity to inspire transference,

[11] Lacan, *The Seminar. Book VIII*, op cit.

Übertragung. That German word coined by Freud to define the particular emotional and intellectual reaction that binds the patient to his psychoanalyst can be translated into Italian with the term *trasporto,* "transfer, transference." Jesus, like Socrates, is a teacher who inspires transference, movement, ignition, re-starting, transport, with the double meaning of "set in motion" and "rouse passion." For example, we can read in those terms all the episodes of resurrection that are strewn through the accounts of the evangelists. Confronted by the dead bodies of the widow's daughter, the centurion, and Lazarus, Jesus always utters the same word: *"Kum!"* "Rise!" Set your life in motion again, begin to live again, start up again!

Jesus is therefore a radical figure of desire.[12] If desire is a force that gets life going, that makes life alive, he is the highest incarnation of that force, such that he literally tears life from the jaws of death, brings life back to life, never lets death have the last word over life. In fact, Jesus presents himself as the one who has come bringing fire ("I am the way, and the truth, and the life"; John 14:6), as the purest embodiment of the Law of desire. While Socrates intends to honor the Law of speech, of discourse, of the *logos,* giving up his life in the name of Truth, Jesus chooses the path of testimony: life is stronger and greater than death, hatred, and destruction. Unlike Socrates, he is the Word who is made flesh, and not the flesh who is sacrificed for the Word.

---

[12] The first to interpret the figure of Jesus starting from the force of desire was Françoise Dolto, *The Jesus of Psychoanalysis: A Freudian Interpretation of the Gospel* (New York: Doubleday, 1979).

Judas and Peter answered the call of Jesus together. They embraced his speech. They presented themselves as students, recognizing in Jesus their common teacher. They are foster brothers; they recognized that a radical truth was operating in that speech. Thus Judas isn't the evil one, isn't the devil, isn't Satan. He was a man in love with his teacher.

Does the trauma of betrayal always imply a disappointment in love? A fall from idealization? Maybe Judas expected from Jesus something that wasn't in Jesus. His idealized love couldn't take account—no idealized love can—of the difference that separates the being of the teacher from the being of the student and what he expects from the teacher. Idealizing love excludes the otherness of the Other and would like that otherness to coincide fully with the narcissistic image of the beloved.

But, more profoundly, Judas appears in the reading of the Gospels as the embodiment of the *political* man. He expected something from his teacher—a politically decisive gesture, a public act on behalf of his people—that never arrived. Did he want Jesus to respond to his demand for the liberation of Palestine from Roman rule?[13] Certainly Judas wanted Jesus' preaching to be politically on the side of the poor and the exploited. There's a scene in the Gospels that is very eloquent from that point of view, and

[13] The historical argument over whether or not Judas belonged to the Zealots (a patriotic-religious movement that interpreted Messianism as the political liberation of the Palestinian land from Roman rule) is controversial and doesn't come within the bounds of my reflections. Cf. Martin Hengel, *The Zealots: Investigations Into the Jewish Freedom Movement in the Period from Herod I until 70 A.D.* (Edinburgh: T & T Clark, 1989).

in which Judas' desire is clearly revealed as the desire of the "political man." The scene takes place at the home of Simon the leper, in Bethany, where a woman takes a jar of pure, very costly ointment and oils Jesus' head. Regarding "this waste" (Mark 14:4), Judas Iscariot objects harshly on political grounds: "Why was this ointment not sold and the money given to the poor? It was worth a year's wages" (John 12:5). We could have given food to the poor rather than delight our teacher with an unnecessary pleasure!

The universal dimension of social justice is central to Judas' political reasoning. Given the need for a more equitable redistribution of wealth, he insists that there can be no compromise. Jesus, however, doesn't seem sensitive— at least in Judas' eyes—to that demand, and disappoints it. He can't be the Palestinian leader of a political movement that calls for social justice. Here is the start of the negative curve of Judas' transference toward his teacher, and the inevitable "de-supposition of knowledge"; that is, as psychoanalysis explains, while the positive transference establishes the teacher as a "subject who is supposed to know," when the transference becomes negative—moves from love to hatred—the fundamental effect is the loss of the supposition of knowledge: the teacher is no longer supposed to have knowledge.[14] Jesus no longer knows what he's doing, he's fallen prey to his narcissistic fantasy, he's lost his ethical compass, he's let himself stray from the path, he thinks only of himself and his image, he lets a woman overwhelm him with kindness, bathe his head with

---

[14] Jacques Lacan, *The Seminar. Book XX. Encore. 1972–1973* (New York: Norton, 1998).

a precious ointment, cover him with tears and kisses, forgetting that his mission is to help the poor and needy. His action diverges from his speech, his gaze is blinded, he has lost his lucidity, he is no longer able to see clearly. In the eyes of Judas, Jesus has betrayed the Cause.

The radical nature of Judas' political criticism should not be underestimated, but, apart from the content of what he proposes, it's tainted at the source; it originates in the wound of the student's disappointed love for the Teacher. In fact, isn't it the anger provoked in him by the "waste" of the woman in Bethany that—as Mark recounts (Mark 14:10–11), and John, too, in his way (John 12:1–11)—sends Judas, the "political man," to hand Jesus over to the chief priests, to sell the life of his teacher, to betray him absolutely? As often happens in relationships between teacher and student, love is converted to hatred. Judas wants the death, the elimination of the one who has disappointed his love. But in his negative transference toward Jesus he seems to have forgotten an essential aspect of his teacher's preaching: the individual, the person, the singularity is *what can't be sacrificed*, and it precedes—comes before—every universal assessment; the truth, that is, has the singular face of our neighbor and not the generic face of humanity or of poverty.

In the house in Bethany, Jesus reiterates the difference between his speech and the political argument. He firmly asks those who criticize him to consider this woman's singular gesture of love, her demonstration that she knows how to really care for him. To the inevitably universal dimension of politics Jesus compares the necessarily singular experience of his own life and his own death:

Let her alone; why do you trouble her? She has done a beautiful thing to me. For you always have the poor with you, and whenever you will, you can do good to them; but you will not always have me (Mark 14:6–7).

The woman has done all she could to alleviate Jesus' increasing pain and anguish. Her love is intense and boundless; her dedication is selfless and generous; her care is an expression of love for the Teacher. She doesn't calculate the cost of her precious ointments, she doesn't evaluate the appropriateness of her act. She loves as women are able to love; her gesture of care is not made anonymously, it's particularized, undertaken as truly exceptional, as an active gift. In fact, a red line connects the woman in Bethany who anoints Jesus' head with a costly perfumed unguent and the widow who gives all she has to the Temple (Mark 12:41–44). Both acts point to a love that has no limits, that skips over the economic calculation, verging on utter extravagance, and that, according to a well-known definition of love proposed by Lacan, "is giving what you don't have." Giving all that she has, the widow offers her utter lack, while those who offer only what is superfluous do not have the experience of lack and, as a result, don't know what love is. So the gesture of the woman in Bethany, which Judas, the "political man," sees simply as a "waste" of resources, as an effect of Jesus' infatuated narcissism, acquires the unique value of a gift, of a generous offering of the self that goes beyond the sterile frame of the useful. The "political man," however, cannot subordinate his universal arguments to the individual name of the subject, as every act of care and love can. Judas remains firm in his conviction:

Jesus betrayed him first, and must in turn be betrayed, so that justice may be done.

Jesus' speech no longer corresponds to Judas' political demand. It is not fully absorbed into the political, as Judas the Zealot would have wished instead. This basic sentiment extends through the story of the woman in Bethany: the disappointment of the student who is betrayed by the teacher. The student can't bear to feel disappointed in the teacher, because he can't bear his otherness, the irreducible freedom of his speech, the disparity between the teacher's being and his own expectations, and therefore, in the last resort, the teacher's vulnerability, humanity, castration.

If, leaving the house in Bethany, Judas decides to sell the life of Jesus, to hand him over to the priests (Mark 14:10–11), it's not an impulsive reaction, an effect of anger. We should, rather, read Judas' decision as the result of a de-supposition of knowledge that has over time worn away his relationship with the Teacher; of a well-thought-out conspiracy; of a real desire to eliminate the teacher's body and his speech, which has become for him a cause for outrage. Whenever a student betrays his teacher, ignoring every form of debt, it's because he no longer recognizes him as a teacher, because he has ceased to nourish himself at his breast, because the teacher's life has become an intolerable shadow that he urgently has to free himself from.

Judas' mind is clouded by the need for autonomy and freedom, and for him their existence depends on the death of the Teacher, on his elimination. This need is the resentful phantom that shadows him. There is no feeling of gratefulness, no gratitude, no perception of the symbolic debt that binds him to Jesus. When Jesus is arrested in the garden of Gethsemane Judas kisses him so that he can be recognized: "And he came up to Jesus at once and said, 'Hail, Rabbi!' And he kissed him" (Matthew 26:49). Even in that final act of greeting ("Hail, Rabbi!") the negative transference of the disappointed student toward his teacher seeps in. Calling him "Rabbi," Judas deliberately intends to ignore Jesus' unique, absolute, incomparable character. He calls him simply "Rabbi," identifying him with other ordinary rabbis. For him Jesus is no longer the Lord, "the way, and the truth, and the life," but a weight he wants to get rid of.

"Do what you came for, friend," Jesus responds (Matthew 26:50). It's the aggressive victory of the student over the teacher. Judas violently upends his relationship as an heir, the symbolic debt that bound him to Jesus. The Teacher is humiliated, removed from his position of teacher, sold, denied, handed over, betrayed. His speech no longer contains any truth; his life isn't worth more than thirty pieces of silver.

PETER'S TEARS

I s the teacher inevitably destined to disappoint his pupils? Is the bond with the teacher always fated to end in patricide? Is it the unconscious desire of every student to destroy his teacher, denigrate his speech, sell him, deny him, betray him?

Judas' betrayal highlights these difficult questions. But hasn't it been said that Judas betrays because he feels betrayed? Because Jesus didn't respond as Judas expected to his political desire? Because he didn't want to subjugate his speech to the needs of the political demand, to free Palestine militarily from Roman rule? The student's betrayal of the teacher is often justified by the feeling that a promise—which the teacher embodies—has been betrayed. And in the eyes of Judas isn't Jesus above all someone who has betrayed a promise?

In the case of Judas disappointed love is transformed into hatred, fidelity into infidelity. Judas isn't Satan, but he is a bad heir. Bad heirs—like the murderous tenants in Jesus' parable—refuse to settle the debt with the owner because they would like to be without debts, the owners of a property that isn't theirs, and absolutely free. They don't want to recognize their lineage. They maliciously interpret inheritance as a violent usurpation. Jesus, as we've seen, indicates that among the murderous tenants are the temple priests, the Pharisees, and the scribes, who have usurped the word of God and won't recognize his son. Here, too, the emphasis is on the betrayal of a symbolic pact. The rebel tenants—like Judas Iscariot—would like to cancel out every form of dependence and debt.

Peter's betrayal is very different. The difference leaps to our eyes immediately: Judas hatches a plot, meditating aggressive revenge on the Teacher who has disappointed him; Peter, on the other hand, betrays out of fear, out of weakness, out of a very human frailty. If for Judas betrayal is experienced not as a gesture of impotence but as the successful outcome of a plan, as a gesture of liberation from a dependency that has become suffocating, for Peter betrayal is a confrontation with his own lack, his complete, helpless unreliability. Peter's betrayal is much more disturbing than Judas'. Because Judas' betrayal coincides with his fate, it's a sort of necessary betrayal, one that is willed, determined, undertaken, while Peter's betrayal clashes with his being, is mainly a betrayal of himself.

For Jesus, the traumatic betrayal is not the negative transference of Judas but the betrayal of the beloved Peter, his most faithful disciple. The true betrayal is not that of the "political man" but that of the student whom Jesus has named as his heir. The true betrayal isn't Judas' but Peter's; the true betrayal is always the betrayal—as it is for Peter—of one's own desire.

After the Last Supper, Jesus and his disciples go out to the Mount of Olives. Judas in the meantime has already sunk. The first words that the Teacher addresses to the disciples who have decided to remain with him are distressing: you will all stumble over me, over my body, "You will all fall away because of me this night" (Matthew 26:31). In Jesus' most difficult hour his disciples will desert him, leaving him alone. They will stumble on the body of their teacher, which has been abandoned, denied, sold. But Peter is the one who reacts with greatest vehemence to Jesus' prophecy, reaffirming his faithful and unassailable love. Not me, certainly not me, I won't be the one who experiences your presence as a reason for falling away. And yet his betrayal is confidently predicted by Jesus, who underscores this prediction by addressing the apostle directly. Your faith is a faith made of straw: "Truly, I say to you, this very night, before the cock crows, you will deny me three times" (Matthew 26:34).

Peter's betrayal is the more painful because Peter was chosen by Jesus as his heir on earth, as the rock that the new community formed in his name will stand on. Jesus announces the imminent betrayal to Peter and to all the disciples: you will be indifferent to my extreme solitude, you will fall away from me, you will deny me, you will stumble on my body.

Peter's act, maybe still more than Judas', even today makes us wonder. Peter is sincere when he declares his love, and he's also sincere when he assures Jesus of his faithfulness. In his words there's no trace of lying, of revenge, of criticism, of hostility; there is no negative transference. His love isn't a disappointed love like Judas'. It's a solid, strong, full, determined love. Unlike Judas, Peter asserts his rock-like faith and the great strength of his love. How much strength do we find in Peter? "If they all stumble over you, if for all the bond with you becomes a reason to fall away, I will never betray you, I will never leave you," he seems to say. "Though all men shall fall away because of you, I will never fall away . . . Even if I must die with you, I will not deny you," Peter states decisively (Matthew 26:32–35).

There is no hesitation in his declaration of love. We should remember the solidity of Peter's faith. It's because of that faith that he, Simon, becomes Peter in the eyes of Jesus. "But who do you say that I am?" he asks his followers once, and, in the astonished silence of the disciples, only Peter can answer without faltering: "You are the Christ, the son of the living God" (Matthew 16:15-16). Peter's strength is the strength of the naked faith that goes beyond any calculation, any program, any strategy. Peter's faith is the faith we find present in every authentic declaration of love. Jesus chooses Peter from among the twelve precisely because Peter is the man of faith: "You are Peter, and on this rock I will build my church, and the powers of death shall not prevail against it" (Matthew 16:18). Peter receives the keys to the Kingdom because of his faith, because of his disinterested love. The trust that Jesus places in him is absolute.

So we should compare these two scenes: the scene of recognition, of full speech that sanctions the One as the disciple of the Other and the Other as the Teacher of the One—Peter recognizes in Jesus the son of God and Jesus recognizes in Peter the rock of his church—with the scene where Jesus announces Peter's imminent triple betrayal. Peter is the man of faith, he is the man whose desire assumes the radical form of naked faith in the Teacher's speech and his promise, his love is strong and pure, yet it is precisely this faith that Jesus reveals as vulnerable and uncertain. Three times before the cock crows, Peter will betray his teacher, will deny him. The offense takes place in front of all twelve: Peter, during the night in Gethsemane, bears a tremendous resemblance to Judas. It's distressing. Jesus has just endured the betrayal of Judas, he has just been sold to the priests, and must immediately endure another insult, the most painful: being betrayed by his most trusted and zealous pupil.

The unfathomable distance that separates Peter from Judas seems to disappear in the thick darkness; the two figures are superimposed. Peter betrays not once but three times, within a few hours. His faith, which seemed made of granite, crumbles, shatters, yields at the first blows, decomposes. How can that happen? Unlike Judas, he doesn't plot, doesn't secretly conspire, doesn't criticize, doesn't ignore but sincerely honors the Teacher's speech. With Peter's betrayal, Jesus dismisses any heroic idealization of faith. He wants to show that even the most solid love—being human—can fall, slide, betray its own object. Doesn't Peter perhaps reflect the dramatic ambivalence that runs through every bond of love? He's speaking the truth when he unhesitatingly declares his love, and yet he is unable to pass the test of this love. His betrayal reveals a contradiction that belongs to the human: we do not always measure up to our love, we are not always consistent with our desire. Is it possible not to measure up, not to be able to pass the tests that love requires? Peter's very human act teaches us that even the purest love, the most determined desire, is fragile and full of contradiction, that, always, human life is exposed to the risk of confusion and disorientation. Nonetheless, the profound difference between Peter's betrayal and Judas' is revealed precisely on this crucial divide and, even in the darkness of the night, prevents us from confusing their outlines. While Judas, faced with the horror of his own act, chooses the path of no return, suicide, Peter weeps. And we have to imagine Peter's tears, we really have to try to imagine Peter's tears. They represent another very human contradiction: between strength and weakness, between the resolute, determined, ardent heart of the disciple named as successor and his frailty, his insecurity, his dividedness. But then Peter's tears are precisely what give his betrayal a different meaning, allowing us to read it in a new light. At the cock's crow, after the third false oath with which he tries not to be identified as a disciple of Jesus by people who had recognized him as such, Peter, realizing the truth of Jesus' prophecy and the betrayal repeated three times, "wept bitterly" (Matthew 26:75). Thus the tears, and not the false speech, the lie, the denial of Jesus, are Peter's final gesture. Those tears are profoundly different from Judas' suicidal act. Those tears keep open a possibility that suicide makes impossible, because in the case of suicide death replaces life and closes off any discourse. Weeping, instead, demonstrates Peter's vulnerable humanity, his lack and his dividedness, and allows him to resume contact with the Other.

Peter's tears teach us something essential about human love. We can always fall into the abyss of betrayal, be inconsistent with our own speech, contradict ourselves, make a mistake, fail, be unfaithful to our own desire. Yet if we are able to recognize our inconsistency, our contradiction, our error, our failure, then our betrayal doesn't obstruct love but establishes love, makes it possible, initiates it. Peter's weeping demonstrates not the end of love but its new beginning after the fall. Ideal love doesn't exist, love without lack and without contradiction isn't part of human life. Most crucial, Peter's tears teach him to welcome his lack, not to reject it, not to deny it, as he denied his teacher. They teach him to make of his lack the new foundation of his love.

UTTER ABANDONMENT

For Jesus, the central experience during the night in Gethsemane is anguish in the face of death. He had never felt it before now. The anguish of death appears for the first time not on the cross but in the solitude of Gethsemane. On that night we see the body of Jesus as we've never seen it before: a body that trembles, weeps, sweats blood, a body crushed by despair. His soul is "overwhelmed with sorrow to the point of death" (Matthew 26:38).

For that reason, Jesus, just like Peter, is tempted by betrayal. He doesn't want to die, he doesn't want to obey his Father's plan; he wants to go on living. His destiny seems to him too heavy: arrest, trial, crucifixion, death. Everything seems intolerable and unjust. Jesus' suffering should be read as the suffering of all human beings confronting their inevitable appointment with death.

Jesus, anguished in the face of death, regrets and exalts the beauty and enchantment of life. We never find in his preaching a spiritualistic or ascetic negation of life; rather, he glorifies life as a gift.[15] And so, because of his

---

[15] On the fundamental nature of Jesus' relationship with the sensual and experiential dimension of life, I would mention, among other possible references, the work that Enzo Bianchi has done on the figure of Jesus. See, for example, his *Gesù e le donne* [Jesus and Women] (Turin: Einaudi, 2016).

attachment to life, his ordeal during the night in Gethsemane turns out to be the exact opposite of the serene experience of the religious martyr or the Greek hero, such as Socrates or Antigone. He appears conflicted, divided, suffering, enveloped in "a mortal sadness," precisely because he doesn't want to die, he doesn't want to sacrifice his life to the Law, precisely because he wants to go on living. His love for the world is too great. All his preaching, as we've seen, has been directed against conceptions of the Law as punitive, requiring sacrifice; it has been aimed at abolishing the Law as weight, oppression, violence against life, at fighting every form of Gnosticism that separates the life of bodies and the world from the life of the spirit and the soul.[16] Nothing is clearer than this: "I have come to abolish all sacrifices and if you will not cease from sacrificing, my anger will not cease."[17]

Jesus' anguish exudes his (anti-sacrifice) passion for life. For those who have tasted the enchantment of life, death is an unnatural act, an intolerable curse. Jesus wants to live because his speech is a speech of life, not death. His tone is fundamentally anti-nihilist. Jesus trembles not at the loss of some thing in the world but at the loss of being in the world. Although, as he repeats, he's not completely *of* the world, he is completely *in* the world (John 17:15–19), while death is the loss of the experience of the

---

[16] I tried to highlight the subversive character of this anti-sacrifice preaching in Recalcati, *Contro il sacrificio,* op. cit.
[17] Mauro Pesce, ed., *Le parole dimenticate di Gesù* [The Forgotten Words of Jesus] (Mondadori: Milan, 2014).

world. Jesus, then, wants to live because he loves that experience and because his speech has glorified it.

Gethsemane is the hour of agony, of helplessness, of utter abandonment, it's the hour of nameless anguish, because it's the hour in which the life of Jesus has to detach itself *from* the world. And here Jesus—like every human being when a trial appears too great—makes his first, very human invocation to his followers: "Stay here and watch with me" (Matthew 26:38). He needs not to feel alone in the night, and asks his dearest friends to stay with him: John, James, and Peter. He doesn't feel he has the strength to bear alone the weight of approaching death. He asks, invokes, claims the presence of his companions, asks his disciples to share the watch, asks not to be left alone. It's not God who makes this entreaty but man. Isn't that request extremely human? Isn't it the same request that anxious children make to their parents when they're afraid of the dark? "Stay here, come sleep with me, don't leave!"

We are struck by this helplessness, displayed in the son of God in its simplest and most dramatic form. Jesus doesn't ask his disciples to save him from his destiny, to find a way to flee, he doesn't ask them to sacrifice themselves in his defense. He would be satisfied if they didn't leave him to bear the weight of that night by himself, if they watched over his tormented sleep. His request is small, but it's evaded just the same. Getting up after losing himself in grief, Jesus realizes that the disciples have left him alone and are sleeping peacefully. At the very moment when their teacher asks them to stay with him, not to abandon him, they fall asleep. His observation is bitter: "So, could you not watch with me one hour?" (Matthew 26:40).

The sleep of the disciples is another image of betrayal. Your brother can't stay near you in the moment of your crisis, your fall, your abandonment. He can't resist sleep. In less than an hour all the disciples are asleep. The flesh (weak) is detached from the spirit (strong). No one is able to share Jesus' solitude and anguish. In fact, this scene, like Peter's betrayal, is also repeated three times.

Peter, James, and John, who were present at the transfiguration of Jesus—at his direct dialogue with God—at his elevation to Heaven, are present now at the fall of Jesus, at his castration. Their teacher is distressed and discouraged, and the horror of death is coming closer and closer. But first he has to endure the painful separation from his brothers, from his students, from human beings. It's the extreme solitude—utter abandonment—that every teacher knows. The students can't tolerate the castration of the Teacher, his imperfection, his humanity. That's why they take refuge in sleep; they don't want to see their Ideal fall in the dust. The time always comes when the team made up of teacher and students breaks down, and there's no one with him as the teacher faces the solitude of his life. The speech of Jesus, who was able to gather people, crowds, who was able to rouse hope in the poor and the disinherited, is no more. During the night in Gethsemane no one is near him. He is compelled to experience absence and solitude precisely at the moment when he is the one asking for help, not the one who is asked for help by those in need. His students don't want to take on the weight of their teacher's solitude. On the boat at the mercy of the storm, as on many other occasions, Jesus saved his followers, who were seized by the fear of death. Then it wasn't the disciples who were dropping off to sleep, as they do during the night in Gethsemane, but Jesus himself. The difference is that for Jesus falling asleep on the boat didn't mean that he left his followers to die. They waked him in anguish: "Teacher, don't you care that we're lost?" And Jesus responded quickly, calming the wind and the sea. But, addressing them, he added a decisive question: "Why are you afraid? Have you no faith?" Isn't it faith that takes away fear in the face of death? Isn't it faith that overcomes the darkest powers?

In the garden of Gethsemane, however, it's Jesus who finds himself at the mercy of the sea and the wind, experiencing the fear of death, but with no one beside him. When the Teacher has lost his glory and is fated to be captured and killed like a common criminal, the disciples leave him alone. They can't even watch over his sleep. They don't want to witness the inevitable loss that Jesus embodies. They want to continue to dream of the Jesus who enters the city of Jerusalem amid the joyful Hosannas of his people. They don't want to witness the death of the Teacher, his profound distance from his Father's Heaven. They don't want to have contact with the wound of the son abandoned by his Father.

JESUS' FIRST PRAYER AND GOD'S SILENCE

Weary and suffering, consumed by anguish, Jesus turns to his father—"Abba, father" (Mark 14:36)—in prayer. For Matthew, he fell with his "face to the ground and prayed" (Matthew 26:39). In this radical way he reveals the essence of speech. The fundamental root of speech is prayer, because—as the act of prayer itself demonstrates—there is no speech that is not an invocation to the Other. Isn't speech ultimately, as Lacan also explains, always an invocation, isn't it always addressed to the Other? In this sense, speech, traumatically silenced in Gethsemane, can reveal its deepest structure, as an opening onto the mystery of the Other, a sacrament of the Other, the Law of the Other.

Jesus' speech has to pass through the difficult bottleneck of silence—the "inhuman" silence of God. Finding himself in the position of invoking the Other, Jesus experiences the fundamental root of speech. But God—his Father—doesn't respond. How is that possible? It's the outrage of Christianity: God can not answer God? And what sort of God is a God who entreats God? A God can pray? The gods don't pray, only men pray. So isn't the figure of the God who prays paradoxical, inconceivable, absurd? Chesterton recalls this when he reports that, on a visit to Jerusalem, a boy guiding him to Gethsemane said: "This is the place where God said his prayers."[18]

Jesus prays not as a God but as a man addressing God experienced as the Father. The most disturbing thing about Gethsemane is God's silence in the face of this invocation. It's the Father's silence in the face of his son's speech invoking him. Thus it's a double silence: the disciples who have fallen into a deep sleep—like the prophet Jonah—and the elusive Father who doesn't hear his son's lament. A tremendous silence opens up between the Teacher and his students and, similarly, between the son and the Father.

When prayer finds no response it takes the form of a cry. In Martin Scorsese's 2016 film entitled, not coincidentally, *Silence*, God, at least up to a certain point in the story, corresponds to an absolute, obstinate silence in the face of the cry and appeal of his followers, martyrs who call on his intervention and their salvation.[19] God responds only with silence. It's the same deafening silence that we encounter

---

[18] G. K. Chesterton, cited in Slavoj Žižek, "The Fear of Four Words: A Modest Plea for the Hegelian Reading of Christianity," in Slavoj Žižek and John Milbank, *The Monstrosity of Christ* (Cambridge: MIT Press, 2009).

[19] In *Silence*, in fact, God does speak, breaking his silence, but only when one of the two young Jesuit missionary monks in Japan, having seen his followers ruthlessly killed, decides to recant to save his own life and that of his brothers who would otherwise die (to no purpose) with him, sacrificed to the Cause. God, in essence, speaks only when the Portuguese monk is able to position life as "unsacrificeable" to any God or any religion, when, in other words, the life of one's "neighbor" is positioned, as such, in the place of God, revealing itself as, precisely, "unsacrificeable." Prayer, therefore, isn't limited to granting the vows of the one praying but modifies his posture profoundly, by allowing him to have another vision of things. Cf. Dietrich Bonhoeffer, *Imparare a pregare* [Learn to Pray] (Magnano, BI: Qiqajon, 2015).

during the night in Gethsemane: God's silence, deafening likewise before the atrocity of the Shoah, or the death of innocent children killed by incurable diseases. In all these cases, and whenever life is subjected to senseless suffering, God's silence seems intolerable and inhuman.

The desperate prayer of Gethsemane also refers to the bloodiest moment of the Passion of Christ crucified. The invocation to God reprises the opening of Psalm 22: "My God, my God, why have you forsaken me?" (Matthew 27:46, Mark 15:34). But the nature of God's silence seems more shocking during the night in Gethsemane because that's when Jesus experiences his Father's silence for the first time in his life. Up until then, his Father had always been near him, had always sustained him, had always answered his appeals. This silence roots Jesus still deeper in man, reveals him, in fact, to be profoundly human, and therefore exposed, like all men, to God's silence.

Jesus prays to the Father asking him to intervene in the Law, to make room for an exception, to consider him truly the only son. Even more: he asks him to contradict his fate, to modify the history that has already been written, to save his singular life from death. The biblical God is in fact the God who can suspend the Law, which is what happens, for example, in the scene of the sacrifice of Isaac: here's a God who speaks and, most important, a God who answers. The biblical God doesn't in the least resemble the gods or oracles of the Greek world, who accept the immutable character of fate; he's a God willing to correct himself, to bend the harshness of the Law to the Law of love.

Jesus prays that he may be allowed to be an exception to what has already been written, an exception to the Law. Might he be revealing his desire in this prayer? Is he failing his vocation? The Jesus who asks for the suspension of the Law (of death) in the name of another Law (of life) is a deeply human Jesus who rejects the inhumanity of the Law.[20] Shouldn't this God who is his father demonstrate that he is reversing his decision to sacrifice his only son to redeem humanity from sin—shouldn't he suspend, as he did with Abraham, the inhuman application of the Law? In the first prayer to the Father, Jesus asks him to change his plan. That entreaty is completely consistent with his preaching: isn't the Law of the Father what it is because it can grasp an exception, can make room for forgiveness, for mercy, can, in short, intervene in the Law? Isn't that what happens countless times in the Gospels: for example in the story of the adulterous woman recounted by John (John 8:1–11), or the figure of the prodigal son in the parable of Luke (Luke 15:11–32)? And isn't that the very task that Jesus imposes in his own preaching: fulfill the Law (Matthew 5:17–20)? Remove the Law from the spirit of revenge, free the Law from the nightmare of sacrifice and punishment in the name of love?[21]

---

[20] Jesus calls men not to a new religion of the Law but to life as "unsacrificeable" in the face of any possible version of the Law. For this reason he prevents the conflict that arises at the moment of his arrest from descending into armed conflict between opposing religions. By urging the disciple (Peter?) who wanted to protect him from the soldiers to put his sword back in its sheath, he demonstrates that the Christian God does not demand any war in his name. Rather, Jesus subjectively takes the step of a giving without reserve, in the name of the Law of his desire. He doesn't want to make others pay for the consequences of his choices. In that sense he can observe his disciples' terrified flight when they're confronted by his killers without calling them back to do anything to defend him.

[21] Cf. Recalcati, *Contro il sacrificio,* op. cit.

JESUS' SECOND PRAYER

In the solitude of Gethsemane, however, there are two fundamental ways for Jesus to understand and practice prayer. One is the plea that he immediately makes to God in his first prayer: release him from draining the bitter cup of his passion to the end, let him go on living, don't require the sacrifice of his life. But, as we know, the son's entreaty is destined to fall into a void. In Gethsemane Jesus occupies the same position as Job: there's no response to his appeal for help, no word from God to break Heaven's silence.[22]

Dietrich Bonhoeffer, in a supremely important letter (included in *Letters and Papers from Prison*), has his own way of looking at the experience of Jesus' prayer in the garden of Gethsemane. His point of departure is that the most profound honesty would consist in a man's agreeing to live fully *in* the world. Not to be completely *of* the world, but to be, still, completely *in* the world. And this being *in* the world—fully in the world—implies the absence of God, an absence that is revealed precisely in Jesus' anguish and prayer. "Christ," Bonhoeffer comments, "helps us not on the strength of his omnipotence but on the strength of his

[22] The relation between Jesus and Job is, not surprisingly, at the center of the reading proposed by Carl Jung, *Answer to Job* (1952; Princeton: Princeton University Press, 2010). On the figure of Christ as a response to Job see also Žižek's observations, "The Fear of Four Words," op. cit.

weakness, his suffering."[23] When Jesus asks his people, "Can't you watch with me?" he is traumatically inverting every theocentric representation of God. No religion can think of God like this. Jesus has the experience of abandonment, betrayal, and an unjust death. His position is the same as Abraham's in the face of God's call; it's the same as Job's in the face of the senseless experience of evil that has no explanation. Not surprisingly, we have in Abraham and Job equally radical, extreme instances of what Jesus is bound to confront during the night in Gethsemane. Jesus asks his father to take away the cup of death; he doesn't ask for the strength to face death—he asks to be freed from it. Jesus isn't Socrates: he doesn't place the *logos* above life.

This, as we've seen, is Jesus' first, very human prayer. But it's not the only way of praying, it's not the only prayer that Jesus makes in Gethsemane. Confronted by God's silence in the face of prayer as entreaty and invocation, he addresses the Father yet again, but this time his posture is different. Jesus' "second prayer" is another form of prayer. The Other's silence has forced him to modify his position, forced him to find the Law in his own heart, not search for the Law in the territory of the Other. In the second prayer he doesn't ask for the Law to be suspended but demands to take it on:

Again, for the second time, he went away and prayed, "My Father, if this cannot pass unless I drink it, thy will be done" (Matthew 26:42).

What establishes the value of speech—as Lacan has

---

[23] Dietrich Bonhoeffer, *Letters and Papers from Prison: Works, Volume 8* (Minneapolis: Fortress Press, 2010).

explained—is not only the level of its statements but the singular (ethical) level of its enunciation. In the second prayer Jesus' enunciation is concentrated in the most profound silence, is fulfilled in the free choice of staying with his own destiny, choosing again, another time, in the face of God's silence, the inheritance that the Father has handed down to him.[24] Jesus seems to have made a dizzying about-face before the hole that the silence has traumatically introduced into the Law. And, rather than call on the Father to intervene in the Law, at the apex of the turn he can subjectify that very intervention by choosing to give his life not to a Law that acts against life but to a Law whose task is to affirm life beyond the Law: to affirm it radically—beyond the Law and beyond death—precisely because it is carried even into death.[25] This is ultimately the

[24] Martin Heidegger, *Being and Time* (1927; New York: Harper & Row, 1962), formulates the paradox of this singular movement: *choosing one's own inheritance.*
[25] Let's recall Jesus' final words on the Last Judgment, which, reported by Matthew, precede the Passion cycle. In this judgment the Son of Man will divide men: on one side those who have been able to "inherit the Kingdom" by welcoming the stranger, the poor, the sick, the thirsty, the hungry; those who have not retreated in the face of the *eteros*, other. On the Lord's right hand, therefore, are the "saved," those who have had experience of lack and love. On the other side, on the Lord's left hand, are the "cursed," those who have not correctly interpreted the inheritance of the Kingdom, who have rejected lack and love. For the former, the face of God is confused with the face of their neighbor; they have seen the Father in the son and God in man. They have done to man what God asks to be done to Him. The others have denied man and therefore denied God, missing the opportunity for the Kingdom. The judgment of the Law seems pitiless, unacquainted with forgiveness. The sin of the "cursed" is not to have loved, to have rejected lack in all its forms. The Last Judgment separates one from the other, the white sheep from the black. The saved are the weaker, or, rather, those who have consolidated a relationship of friendship with lack, the most vulnerable (Matthew 25:31–46). We might perhaps make this image secularly more elastic, and consider the border separating the two not so much a rigid, segregating barrier but a place of transition, of passage, such that we can be first on one side and then on the other, or, rather, that being on one side or the other is not a condition of being but only a mode of existence.

direction that his prayer takes. He responds to the Father's silence not with atheistic hatred or resigned disillusionment, not with religious belief or, finally, the entreaty of the first prayer. In fact, the new prayer is made possible precisely by God's silence; it's Jesus' final response to God's silence. He doesn't want to break that silence; he wants to emerge from it. The frustration of the first, entreating prayer generates the possibility of the second prayer. That's why Bonhoeffer can write, paradoxically, that the atheist—who experiences the absence of God, his silence—is much closer to God than the man of faith, because the "God who is with us is the God who abandons us." And for this reason, Bonhoeffer continues, "being Christian doesn't mean being religious, it means being man."[26]

Jesus in Gethsemane—like Job but *beyond* Job— undertakes prayer as a commitment to the mystery of God rather than to his speech. This doesn't mean promoting the sacrifice of oneself, it doesn't subjugate life to the duty of the Law, but, faced with the ordeal of death, he places his trust in the inscrutable will of the Father: "Not what I will, but what thou wilt" (Mark 14:36); "Not my will, but thine, be done" (Luke 22:42). But what does this ultimate commitment mean? Jesus is handed over or hands himself over to the will of the Father? Does he submit to being handed over or does he experience it as a task that defines his life? Bread and wine are the body and blood of Christ. But does becoming the paschal "lamb" mean being sacrificed on the sacrificial altar? Does shedding one's blood

---

[26] Bonhoeffer, *Letters and Papers from Prison,* op cit.

correspond to an act of expiation or to a donation that turns out to be overabundant? Is the paschal sacrifice truly a sacrifice? Can the gift of bread and wine, or of one's own body, really be reduced to a sacrificial device, an openly masochistic phantom?[27]

"My time [*kairos*] is at hand," Jesus declares (Matthew 26:18) just before the start of the Passion. He wants to change the way the Law is understood; he doesn't feel he's subject to a Law that doesn't respond and doesn't forgive, but finds, ultimately, in himself his own Law, the Law of his own desire. Jesus, as Paul writes, doesn't suffer death but *gives himself* (Galatians 2:20) to the Law. In this subtle but profound difference, Jesus' act is not at all an act of sacrifice but one that, starting on the night in Gethsemane, well before the torture of the arrest, the trial, Calvary, and Crucifixion, frees the Law from the deadly shadow of sacrifice.

In the second prayer Jesus overturns his relationship with the Law: he adopts the Law as the truth of his own desire without further subjecting himself to its violence. Obedience to the Law coincides with obedience to his own desire. This is the unprecedented swerve introduced by the second prayer. Jesus frees himself from waiting for a response from the Other, and from belief in the existence of the Other of the Other as the Other who responds. He can thus pass through the phantom of the first Law—punitive, requiring sacrifice—to reach a new version of the Law: the gift of himself, of taking on the Law of his own desire.

---

[27] It's the glaring error that Lacan, unfortunately, in his reading of the Passion of Christ, commits. *The Seminar. Book X*, op cit.

But while he has pledged to complete this difficult and decisive swerve, he walks toward his disciples, who should have been nearby watching over him, and finds them asleep yet again: "When he came back, he again found them sleeping, because their eyes were heavy" (Matthew 26:43). This underlines the fact that only in the most complete solitude (abandoned by God and by his disciples) can Jesus truly work this new introjection of the Law. For all practical purposes, it's a matter of testimony: he shows what a Law can be that is different from the Law imposed on man like an oppressive yoke, but also different from the wait for the Law as a response from the Other. At stake is the existence of a Law that requires obedience not to its will to death or to the response from the Other but to the subject's most radical desire, which coincides with the otherness of the fate that inhabits us, or rather with its entrustment to the Other. To hand one's life over to one's own desire doesn't mean only freeing the Law from the "ought" as the sacrifice of our own being but also welcoming the absence of God, atheism, as the condition in fact of man, the nonexistence of the Other of the Other, of the Other who responds. It means understanding that being handed over to the Other is one of the fundamental ontological structures of human life.[28]

My life is handed over to itself, to the otherness that inhabits it, to its ethical task, to the Law, and to the transcendence of its own desire. In this sense Jesus *gives*

---

[28] Emmanuel Levinas, in a close reading of the biblical text, has perhaps more than anyone else developed this theme of being handed over, delivered, to the Other. See, for example, Emmanuel Levinas, *Nine Talmudic Readings* (Bloomington: Indiana University Press, 1990).

himself to his being given, decides to entrust himself to his own fate, submits to the will of the Father. His responsibility consists in transforming the drive to sacrifice into an act of giving himself fully. It's a dizzying passage: he doesn't simply experience the predictive power of the Scriptures—"everything was already written"— but produces a new scripture: *accepting that his life has been handed over, he frees it from being handed over.*

This may be the most important lesson of the night in Gethsemane. Jesus' second prayer is the result of a *complete disarming*. The I submits to an otherness that overwhelms it, and accepts the law of desire as fate. That's why the "beautiful thing" of the woman in Bethany is worth more than all that his disciples do. While she recognized that the life of Christ had been "handed over" and offered it everything she possibly could, uncalculatingly, unsparingly, the traitor, supported by other disciples, encouraged political criticism. Jesus behaves just like that woman: he offers up the life that he loves infinitely in an excessive, subversive, boundless gesture of giving. In the thick darkness of night in Gethsemane, he pays no attention to the cost of his act but only to the act, to the absolutely inherent value of his act.

To free man from the fear of death and from the interpretation of the Law as sacrifice a final step is needed. Jesus prays, and in his second prayer he grasps an ultimate truth: it's a matter not of asking for the suspension of the Law but of *placing one's trust in the Law that is the Law of the Father beyond sacrifice*. Faith arises not because God sends "signs"—as Paul would say—or because his presence and his severe gaze instill fear, but precisely because he is absent and doesn't respond. That is the extreme paradox that is revealed in the garden of Gethsemane while all the disciples remain shut in their deep sleep and Judas the traitor sells Jesus to the temple priests.

The most deep-rooted faith arises not from the presence of God but from his absence. That's why, as I've already noted, Bonhoeffer can write that those who are "without God" are closer to God. The atheist who doubts, who has a profound experience of solitude, resembles Jesus in Gethsemane more than the believer who doesn't know the drama of doubt. To be Christian, Bonhoeffer constantly reminds us, doesn't mean placing our trust in religion; it means simply to be men, to have the experience of the nonexistence of the Other of the Other, of the absolute silence of God.[29]

Gethsemane teaches us that being without God means being closer to God, and that the experience of God's absence paradoxically brings God closer to man. But that closeness isn't simply consoling. In it we find, rather, the most profound experience of prayer. The height of prayer isn't the ego's recovery of strength in order to endure a difficult trial but an unconditional act of disarming, of handing over, of offering, beyond the ego.

"Not my will, but yours, be done," Jesus concludes his time of anguish. Thus the ego yields, retreats, places its trust in the Other, even though the Other—and this is the ultimate trial—doesn't answer. God is not present in Gethsemane in any way, except in the form of his most

[29] Bonhoeffer, *Letters and Papers from Prison*, op cit.

profound absence. Only in Luke does an angel sent by God appear, as if in an extreme gesture of *pietas*, to console his son (Luke 22:43). A vestige of Heaven that falls to earth, a residue of the vanished presence of the great Other.

About the Author

Massimo Recalcati is a psychoanalyst and author who teaches at the universities of Pavia and Verona. His many books have been translated in several languages. He lives and works in Milan.